MODEL A FORD CLUB

CAPE HENRY

1928-1931

This book is dedicated to all the helpful members of
The Cape Henry Model A Ford Club for keeping Lady Lilli on the road.

A special thanks to her godfathers:
Dick Eberle and Dave Curl, who welcomed us into the club.

Author Melanie Kordis first met Lady Lilli in 2013 and they have enjoyed many adventures together. In addition to writing *Lady Lilli Has One Horn*, Melanie writes the monthly Fashion and Life column for the Cape Henry Model A Ford Club newsletter. When not adventuring, Lady Lilli spends her time in a well-appointed garage painted straw yellow to match her wheels.

Young children will recognize numbers.

Young readers will be introduced to a new vocabulary and a simplified explanation of how parts work.

All readers can participate in preserving American history and ingenuity.

Readers are welcome to send an email to LadyLilli.adventures@gmail.com

Model A's had several body styles and were used as passenger cars, service cars and working trucks. The body or frame of the Model A came in several different colors; however, ***the fenders always came in black.***

Drivers of classic cars needed to know about how their cars worked. Many people did not live in a city where their cars could be repaired by a mechanic. The Model A years (1928 - 1931) were during the time of the Great Depression (1929 - 1938). Many car owners did not have the money to have their cars repaired and relied on their own skill. Drivers checked their cars before getting on the road and often carried extra parts for repairs. Lady Lilli wants her readers to know more about how she runs so that you can enjoy her adventures and help her if she breaks down on the road.

AHOO

Lady Lilli has ONE horn.

The Ahooga blast coming from her horn is iconic and easy to recognize. The actual sound is created by the horn's electric motor spinning a metal plate. The motor speeding up and slowing down changes the pitch of the horn. The "ah" sound is created when the motor speeds up. The "oo" sound is when the motor is at maximum speed. The "ga" sound is when the motor slows down.

2

Lady Lilli has TWO headlights.

There are two settings. A high beam setting and a low beam setting. The high beam casts the light rays upward for greater visibility down the road. The low beam casts the light rays downward as not to distract motorists driving on the other side of the road.

Lady Lilli has THREE forward gears.

The gears are controlled by a sliding gear transmission. The driver manually moves the transmission shift lever with their right hand while depressing the foot clutch pedal with their left foot. The gear shift is arranged in the classic "H" pattern:

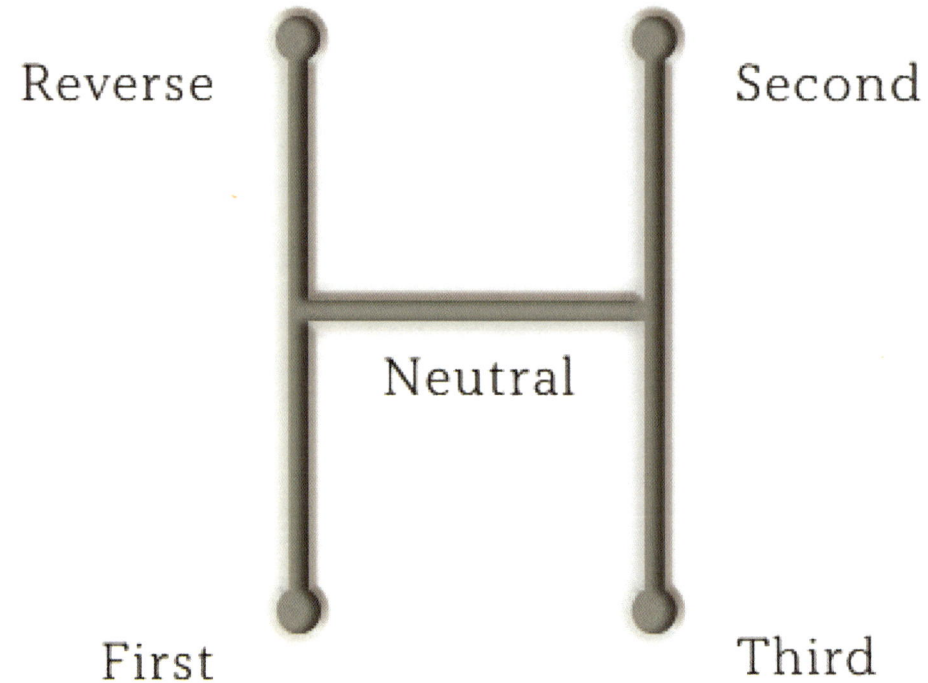

Reverse

Second

Neutral

First

Third

Lady Lilli has FOUR spark plugs.

Spark plugs produce an electric spark. Electricity is needed to start her internal combustion engine. The electricity originates from a six-volt battery and travels through wires to a distributor and then into each spark plug.

Lady Lilli can accommodate FIVE riders.

The driver and a passenger in the front seat and up to three passengers in the back seat. Convertible models such as the Cabriolet or Roadster do not have a back seat. They have a rumble seat, also known as a chaperone's seat.

When the rumble lid of the car is opened, passengers have access to the rumble seat by climbing up the two steps mounted above the bumper and on the right rear fender. The rumble seat can be very cozy!

Lady Lilli has SIX wheels.

Two wheels are additional and ready to use as spares. Carrying one or two spare wheels was a good idea back in 1930. Tires of the time were of poor quality, and unpaved roads placed a lot of wear and tear on the tires. Motorists expected flat tires on their journey and needed to change them alongside the road.

When Lady Lilli came from the factory, she had her own pouch of tools so the driver or a fellow traveler could change the tire without too much delay.

Lady Lilli requires a sequence of SEVEN steps to start her engine:

One: Make certain the gas valve is open
Two: Retard the spark lever
Three: Advance the throttle lever
Four: Shift into neutral
Five: Turn the ignition key
Six: Pull the choke with your right hand and
Seven: Press the starter button with your right foot

And away we go!

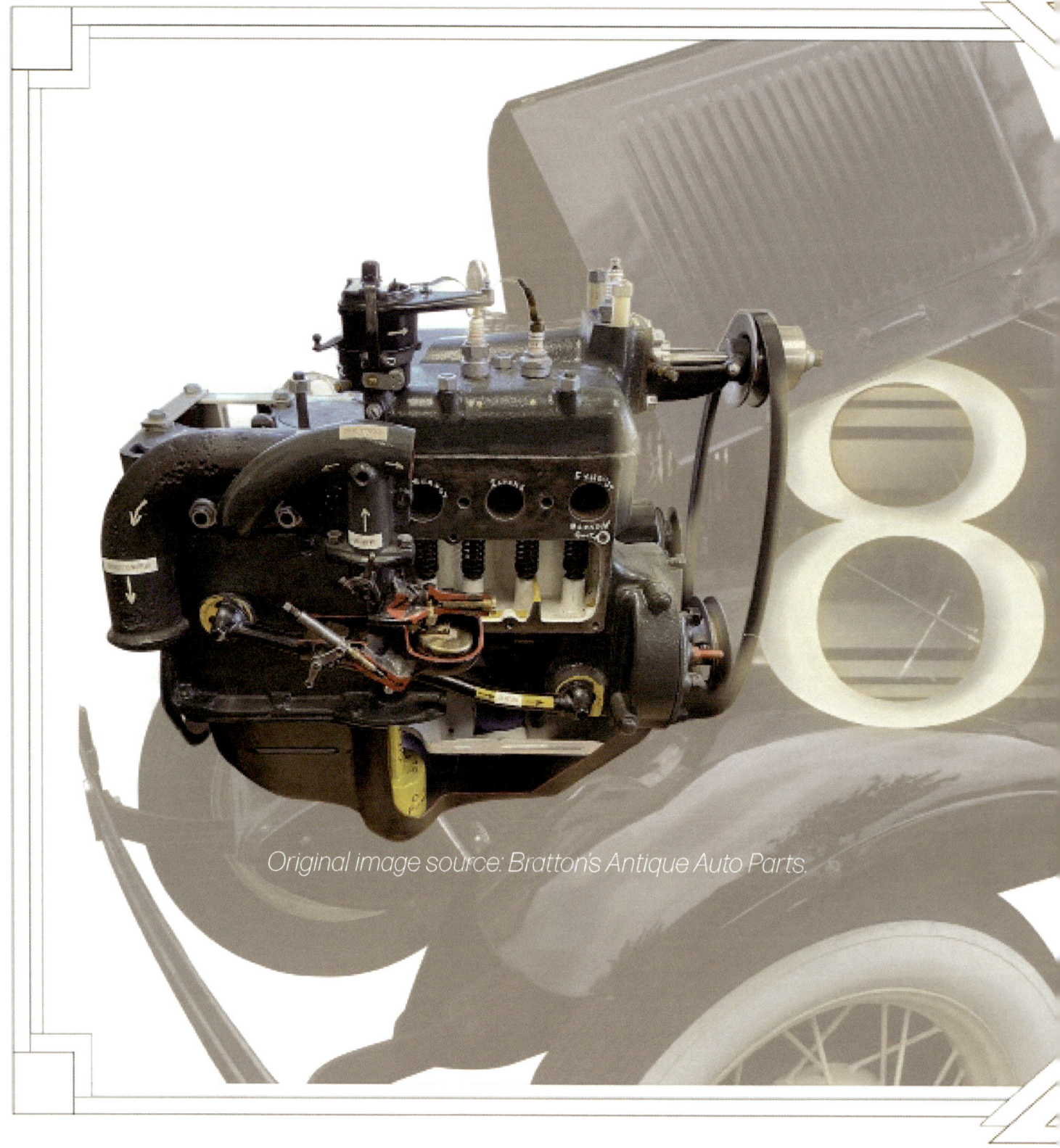

Original image source: Bratton's Antique Auto Parts.

Lady Lilli's internal combustion engine has EIGHT mechanical parts:

crankshaft

pistons

piston rods

intake valves

exhaust valves

spark plugs

timing gears

camshaft

These mechanical parts move in a synchronized order. The movement creates a chemical reaction when fuel, air, and electricity are added. The energy produced by the mechanical movements and chemical reaction makes Lady Lilli go.

Lady Lilli and other Model A's were assembled in NINE countries in addition to many cities in the United States of America.

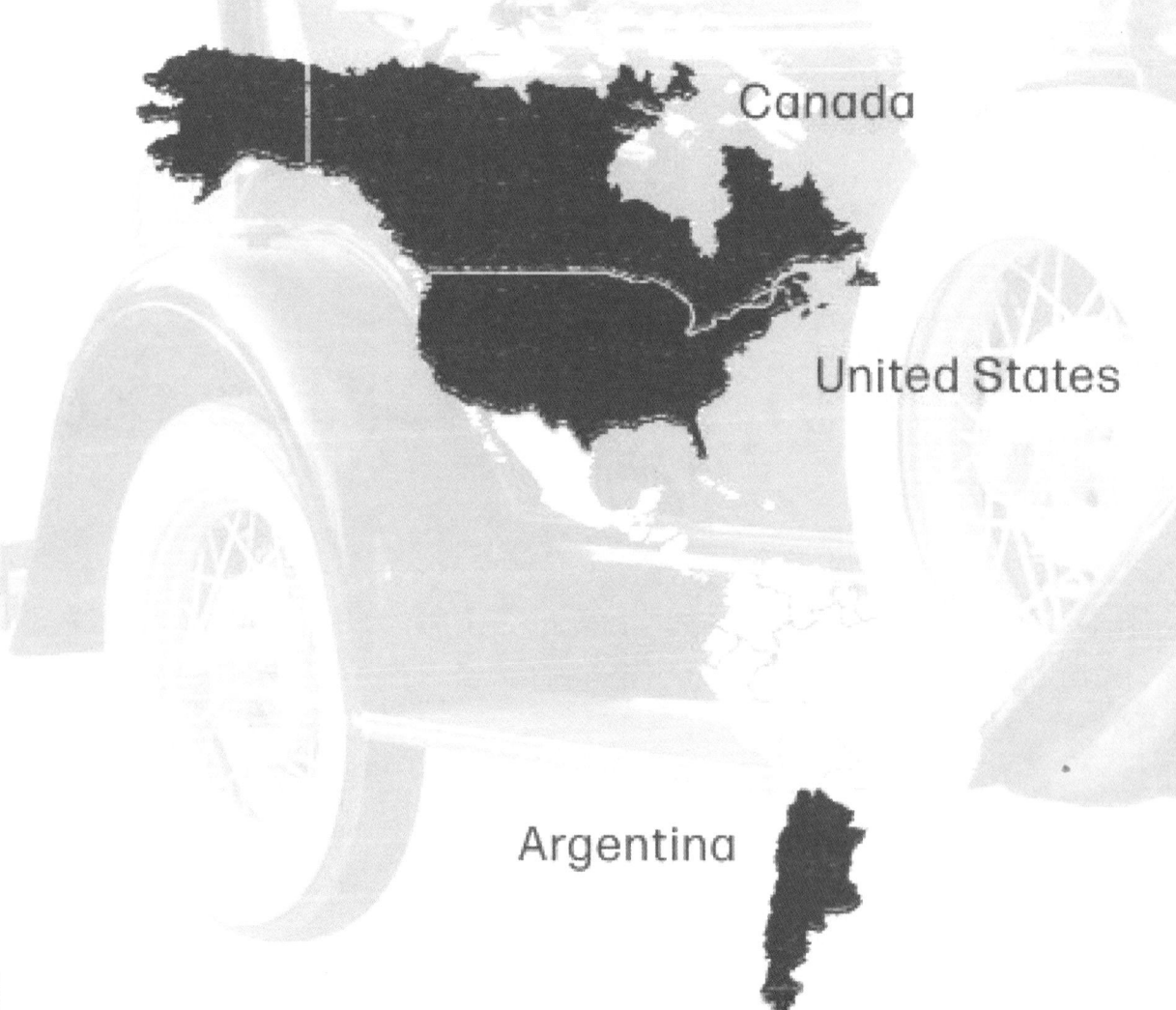

Canada

United States

Argentina

9

United Kingdom
Denmark
Germany

Italy

France

Japan

Lady Lilli's predecessors
(Model A's built in 1928 and 1929)
had fuel tanks that could hold TEN gallons of gas.

The 1930 and 1931 models could hold up to eleven gallons of gas.
Mr. Henry Ford, inventor and builder, knew that the gas gauge may not
always read correctly. Before any automobile left the factory, the gauge was
adjusted to read zero "0", even though there was still at least one-half gallon
of gas left in the tank.

Lady Lilli's Next Adventure

Join Lady Lilli and friends on a country road adventure.
They will be visiting farm stands in Virginia, carrying
home fresh-picked berries for pies, preserves and tasty
vegetables for side dishes and soups.

Recipes Included!